SOPRINTENDENZA ARCHEOLOGICA DI ROMA

THE NATIONAL ROMAN MUSEUM
PALAZZO MASSIMO ALLE TERME

ELECTA

THE NATIONAL ROMAN MUSEUM LOCATED IN PALAZZO MASSIMO ALLE TERME

Palazzo Massimo alle Terme gets its name from the noble Roman Massimo family, who were the owners of villa Peretti Montalto during the last century. This was once the private villa of cardinal Felice Peretti (later to become Pope Sixtus V, 1585-90), and stood on the Viminale facing the Esquiline, next to the monumental ruins of the Diocletian's Thermae.

During the 16th century this villa, adorned with buildings of great architectural value, was among Rome's most beautiful and was praised for its splendid gardens and large collection of ancient works of art. In the 18th century it became the property of the Negroni family and by the end of the century was largely stripped of all its furnishings and ancient works. In 1789 the Massimos took possession of the villa but it was gradually torn down, starting in 1860, coinciding with the construction of the new Termini Railroad Station.

In 1883, in the area still owned by the Massimos, the Jesuit Massimiliano Massimo began the construction of a stately building, designed by the architect Camillo Pistrucci. The structure, which was inspired by late 16th century architecture, was finished in 1887 and was situated next to the 16th century villa's main edifice, which bore the name "di Termini". In 1888 the latter was confiscated and demolished in conjunction with the expansion of the new station.

The central façade of this imposing six-storey building overlooked the station's square, and the narrow entrance faced Largo di Villa Peretti. It became the seat of the Jesuit college "Massimiliano Massimo", and preserved that function until 1960. Many illustrious italian personalities belonging to the world of culture have studied there, including the architect Clemente Busiri Vici, the archeologist Enrico Paribeni and the writer Ignazio Silone.

In 1960 the Massimo Institute vacated the building and moved to his new location in E.U.R. and the italian government subsequently bought the structure in 1981, restructuring and annexing it to the National Roman Museum in the Diocletian's Thermae. This museum was originally founded in 1889 (together with the National Etruscan Museum in Villa Giulia) in the structures belonging to the Carthusian convent of Santa Maria degli Angeli and the Roman Thermae, and was destined to house both the antiquities from the Kircherian Museum (then part of the collection belonging to the Roman College), and archeological material dating back to the Roman period. These archeological finds were unearthed in Rome and its surroundings after 1870, when the official capital of the Unified Realm of Italy was moved to its present site.

The constant discovery of new finds that took place during this century rendered the historical site at the Diocletian's Thermae and the

1. View of the the inner courtyard

convent of the Carthusians inadequate. Additional space was needed, not only for more articulated exhibition areas, but also for the installation of various services that were deemed necessary for the running of a modern museum.

Using funds made available by a special law for the tutelage of the Roman archeological patrimony (1981), it was possible to carry out the expansion of the National Roman Museum in this new location, which was restored by the architect Costantino Dardi. The

restoration was done during the Eighties and it comprised not only four floors of museum space but also offices, a library, a conference room, archives and a computerized documentation center.

The first three floors in the Museum house the *Ancient art section* and in 1995 the ground floor exhibit was opened to the public. In 1998 the remaining first and second floor installations were completed, as well as the underground floor which houses the *Numismatic and jewelry section*.

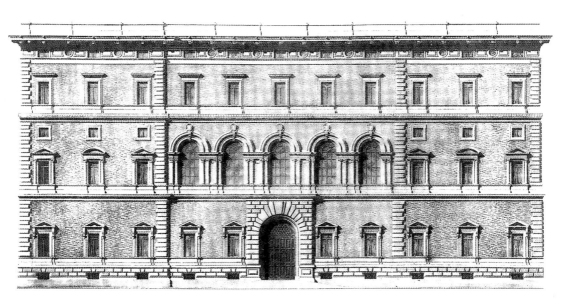

2. The main façade of
Camillo Pistrucci's
building plan

ANCIENT ART SECTION

The *Ancient art section*, which occupies the ground, first and second floors in the new location, contains the most significant works of art produced between the end of the republican age (II - I century BC) and the late imperial age (IV century AD), together with some original Greek works from the V century BC; the exhibition describes not only the artistic activities that were being carried out in ancient Rome, but also the political and economic context in which they developed and their historical evolution.

GROUND FLOOR

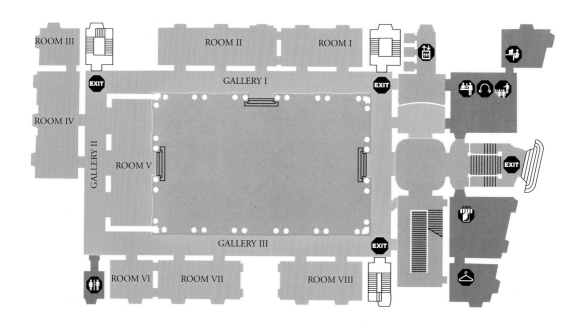

GALLERY I
**Portraits from
the republican period**

ROOM I
**Image and celebration
from the period between
Sulla and Caesar**
(*Laus auctoritatis*)

ROOM II
**Image and celebration
during the period between
Caesar and Augustus**
(*Laus auctoritatis*)

GALLERY II
The imperial cult

ROOM III
Money and power
(*Signum rei publicae*)

ROOM IV
**The Empire's ideology
The Julius-Claudii**
(*Imago imperii*)

ROOM V
The ideology of power
(*Augustus*)

GALLERY III
**Reconstructed
Greek portraits**

ROOM VI
**Power and the Arts
The models**
(*Exemplaria artis*)

ROOM VII
**Power and the Arts
The originals (*Graecitas*)**

ROOM VIII
**Power and the Arts
The figurative language**
(*Amoenitas artis*)

Access to the Museum is through the main entrance on Largo di Villa Peretti; a plaque on the left wall of the stairs, placed there by ex-pupils of the "Collegio M. Massimo" in 1993, commemorates the restoration of the building.

In the passageway beyond the ticket office there's a statue of Minerva seated. It's a large polychrome sculpture executed in white marble, alabaster and basalt. The face is a modern plaster cast of another head of the same deity, the so-called "of the Athena Carpegna" type (likewise exhibited in the same area). This large cult statue, (inspired to statues in different materials typical of Greek and Magna Graecia art of the V century BC) discovered at the foot of the Aventine hill, may have been part of a temple dedicated to this goddess and built on the hill sometime around the end of the I century BC or the beginning of the I century AD.

The ground floor exhibition consists of eight rooms, which surround a vast central courtyard, and three galleries.

GALLERY I
Portraits from
the republican period

The ten portraits on exhibition here may have originally served funerary or honorary functions and they show the evolution of taste in Roman society during the last part of the republican age (between the end of the II and the end of the I century BC). The layout evokes those "family picture galleries" which preserved the ancestors' features, instilling among their descendants the virtues of those belonging to the noble class.

Displayed on the wall at the end of the corridor is a mosaic floor from the triclinium of a suburban villa on Via Labicana, in the area of Tor Bella Monaca. It dates back to the I century AD and has a small central square (*emblema*) made from tiny mosaic tiles which dates back to the preceding age (II - I century BC) and depicts the myth of the abduction of the young boy Hylas by the Nymphs.

ROOM I
Image and celebration from
the period between
Sulla and Caesar
(*Laus auctoritatis*)

Near the entrance of this room we find the Fasti Anziati (*Fasti Antiates maiores consulares et censorii*), calendars of great epigraphic importance painted on plaster. They are dated back between 84 and 55 BC and were discovered among the ruins of Nero's villa in Anzio. They consist of a calendar of holidays earlier than that instituted by Caesar, and a list of magistrates, specifically consuls and censors, holding office between 173 and 67 BC.

on the previous page:

*3. Head of Athena,
known as "Athena
Carpegna"*

*4. Mosaic emblem showing
Hylas and the Nymphs*

*5. Portrait of an old woman
from Palombara Sabina.
Late-republican age*

6. Statue-portrait of the so-called General from Tivoli.
The statue, in pentelico marble, was found among the ruins of the structures of the Temple of Hercules the Victor in Tivoli and is typical of a late-hellenistic technical process of working parts separately. It's one of the most significant works of Roman art belonging to the I century BC and it is surely of Greek workmanship. It depicts an older man belonging to the ruling class, perhaps a general (as suggested by his armor), who took part in the victorious military campaigns in Asia between 90 and 70 BC. Regardless of various hypotheses however, no one has been able to identify this personage

The main theme of this exhibit, which can be seen in these portraits of the upper classes, is the variety of ideologies found among members of Roman society. These portraits of members of the ruling class of Rome and other municipalities (Palestrina, Mentana), show either the persistence of the etruscan-italic artistic tradition or a style similar to the one shown in portraits of hellenistic princes.

The statue-portrait of the so-called General of Tivoli (circa 70 BC) shows the glorification of his military virtues by depicting him in heroic nudity, in accordance with the models of classical Greek sculpture, yet at the same time contains a moving and concentrated personal portrait.

ROOM II
Image and celebration during the period between Caesar and Augustus (*Laus auctoritatis*)

The funerary steles and portraits shown in this room belong to the critical historical period (second half of the I century BC) that witnessed the rise of Caesar and the successive struggles for power that ended in Mark Antony's defeat by Octavian. The emergence of new social classes is in evidence, especially among freedmen of foreign origin (mostly Greek): the typology of the funerary steles engraved with family portraits, the dead represented in togas, shows that the acquisition of Roman citizenship represented a widespread value among these groups, which were also economically relevant.

At the far end of the room there is a calendar engraved on marble slabs, the so-called *Fasti Praenestini*, which were originally installed in the forum of the town of Palestrina (*Praeneste*) by the magistrate Verrio Flacco, and which demonstrate how the Cae-

---

7. Funerary relief of the Rabirii.
This relief was originally part of a wall in one of the various graves found along the Via Appia. The deads portrayed on this relief and commemorated with inscriptions are

C. Rabirius Hermodorus and Rabiria Demaris, both probably of Greek origin, judging from their names, and freedmen of an illustrious personage from the caesarean age, C. Rabirius Postumus. The third person

represented here, on the right, is their descendant Usia Prima, known as "priestess of Isis". Her figure was added to the relief at a later date by modifying a male bust in toga. Her hairstyle is also indicative of a following period

(I century AD). The sistrum and patera in the background are symbols of the Egyptian cult of the goddess Isis

sarean calendar was altered by Augustus.

GALLERY II
The imperial cult
This gallery contains a statue of an emperor in military dress, unrecognizable because of the missing head, but attributable to the II century AD for stylistic reasons, and two inscriptions from the augustan age which illustrate the homage rendered to the emperor (the façade of an altar with a dedication to *Lares Augusti* and part of another altar with a sacred dedication in favour of Augustus).

ROOM III
Money and power
(*Signum rei publicae*)
This room contains a coin collection that illustrates the development of minting on Ita-lian soil. In Rome, money du-ring the republican age made use of the monetary traditions of the cities of Magna Graecia and Sicily and developed thanks to political competition between the great families and between the magistrates. Above all, with the emergence of the great leaders of the late republican age (Marius, Sulla, Pompeus, Caesar) money became a means of propaganda; using this model, money issued during the reigns of Augustus and the other emperors belonging to the Julius-Claudia family was a valid in-

strument for the transmission of propagandistic images and concepts that served to reinforce the power of the leader.

ROOM IV
The empire's ideology
The Julius-Claudii
(*Imago imperii*)
Numerous portraits of high artistic quality, executed in both marble and bronze, are

found in this room. They were made between the augustan age and the middle of the I century AD. For the most part they represent members of the imperial family: a youthful portrait of Octavian, done before the victory of Azio (31 BC) and of the final conquest of power; portraits of his sister and his wife, Octavia and Livia; portraits of some of the princes designated as his successors (Germanicus, Druso Maggiore) and his actual successors (Tiberius, Caligula). There are also portraits of private citizens, in which one can see how the images of the emperor and his family influenced portraiture of the time.

The room also contains inscriptions on marble slabs that form the base for statues of Augustus, Nero, Claudius and Agrippina Minore, as well as a bronze inscription on the base of a statue dedicated to Tiberius in 7 BC, and a marble head of a private citizen, discovered in a sacred area that was recently excavated at the foot of the Palatine near the Arch of Constantine; an *aedicula* dedicated to the imperial religion by a musician's college was also found.

8. Didracma with the head of Hercules on the obverse and the wolf nursing the twins on the reverse side. First half of the III century BC

an end to civil wars and restoring public affairs (*res publica*) to the Senate and the Roman people, as if he were a second Romulus. Although he ruled under the aegis of a republican form of government, his deeds were actually more in keeping with those of a monarchy.

In the statue from the Via Labicana, Augustus, draped in a toga, appears in his capacity of *Pontifex Maximus*. The exaltation of ancient Roman sacerdotal offices serves to accentuate Augustus' religiosity (*pietas*).

Even the exaltation of the legends relative to the birth of Rome and therefore the Trojan myth (transposed into Virgil's epic poem, the Aeneid, precisely during the Augustan principality), represents one of the principal cultural and religious trends of Augustus' age.

At the base of augustan political policy was the desire to recover the traditional values inherent in Roman identity, and the frescoes from a tomb on the Esquiline are evidence of this policy. Dating from the caesarean or protoaugustan period, these frescoes contain scenes from Trojan and Romulean legends which deal with the origins of Rome. Similar themes can be found in the decorations on an altar from Ostia, which presents not only the so-called "lupercale" (Romulus and Remo nursed by a wolf) but also the

ROOM V
The ideology of power (*Augustus*)
This room represents the central concept of the ground floor exhibition and contains works symbolizing the ideology which influenced and justified the political and cultural choices of the augustan principality (27 BC - 14 AD). Octa-

vian, son of a Knight but Caesar's descendant on his mother's side and adopted by that family, seized power after having defeated Antony and Cleopatra at Azio. In 28 BC, he assumed the title of *Augustus* ("he who grows"). He presented himself to the Senate as the savior of the country and claimed credit for having put

9. Portrait of Livia. Images of Livia, emperor Augustus' wife, decidedly influenced all private portraiture of the period, both for the idealized style of her portraits and her hairstyle. Other empresses portraits

would subsequently have the same influence over female contemporaries portraits. Here her hair, parted in the center, are gathered in a frontal knot and in a group of braids situated on the nape of her neck; both of these elements are

attached to each other by a connecting braid. The almond-shaped eyes, aquiline nose and small thin lips are typical of the empress' facial features

10. Statue of Augustus
from the Via Labicana.
Augustus is portrayed
wearing a tunic and an
ample toga which is also
pulled up over his head
in the Italic tradition.
His face, bearing an
intense and grave
expression, shows evident
influences of hellenistic
princes portraits. This
portrayal, which could
be posthumous, shows
Augustus in the guise of
Pontifex Maximus, the
high religious position he
assumed in 12 BC. Even
the recovery of ancestors'
religious values in the
augustan ideology
becomes a political
instrument to justify the
establishment of a
dynastic cult

11. Frescoes from the colombarium on the Esquiline.
This frieze was found on the Esquiline and decorated a sepulchral chamber (starting on the right wall and running to the left) which belonged to the Statilii family and was part of the necropolis of the Esquiline. It contains scenes illustrating the Trojan and Romulean legends and dates back to the second half of the I century BC. The inscriptions were initially legible but have now almost completely disappeared. It shows a succession of scenes, painted in a refined hellenistic technique, that includes battle scenes between Trojans and Rutuli, the construction of city walls (perhaps Lavinio), other battle scenes between Trojans and Rutuli, the construction of another city wall (perhaps Alba Longa), a meeting between two military leaders and an interior with female figures. One can also make out the scene of the encounter between Mars and Rhea Silvia and her subsequent conviction by king Amulio, who had forced her to become a vestal virgin. The last scene of the frieze shows the twins Romulus and Remus in a basket, on the Tiber, surrounded by a characteristic pastoral landscape

West wall.
From the right:
a. Scene of city foundation.
b. War between Rutuli and Trojans.

Long south wall.
From the right:
a. Battle of the Numico River and Apotheosis of Aeneas.
b. Truce between Ascanio and Mezenzio.
c. Scene of city foundation.
d. Interior with female figures.

Long west wall.
From the right:
a. Consecration of Rhea Silvia as a vestal virgin.
b. Amorous encounter between Mars and Rhea Silvia.
c. Condemnation of Rhea Silvia.

North wall.
From the right:
a. Imprisonment of Rhea Silvia.
b. Exposure of the twins on the banks of the Tiber.
c. Prodigy of the Lupercale (...).

12. *Altar from Ostia.
This marble altar,
attributed to the age of
emperor Trajan, comes
from Ostia and is
dedicated to the divine
couple Mars and Venus.
The inscription
indicates that it was re-
used in Hadrian's age
as the base of a statue
dedicated to the god*

*Silvan. The main
façade illustrates the
sacred wedding of the
two deities: Mars
fathered Romulus,
founder of Rome and
son of Rhea Silvia;
Venus was the mother
of Aeneas (and
pregenitress of the gens
Iulia, to which Julius
Caesar belonged), the*

*Trojan hero who
united his people with
the Latins, giving
origin to Roman
progeny. On the lateral
sides "eroti", belonging
to the goddess
procession, are depicted
playing with Mars'
weapons and coach.
The rear façade
represents the*

*"lupercale" (Romulus
and Remus nursed by
the wolf) surrounded
by personifications of
the Tiber and the
Palatine*

b   *a*

d   *c*   *b*

c   *b*

c

a

a

b　　　　　　　　　　　　　　　　　　　*a*

guardian deities of Rome, Mars and Venus.

GALLERY III
**Reconstructed
Greek portraits**
On the wall at the beginning of the corridor is a mosaic floor that comes from a I century BC suburban villa discovered along the Via Ardeantina. The central square (*emblema*) is finely made in a technique that characterizes hellenistic work-manship during the II century BC. It depicts a wild cat biting a bird and in the lower register two ducks. These themes can be found in other mosaics from the same period.

Eight portraits of Greek personages are displayed along the gallery, clearly showing the influence that Greek classical culture and iconography had on Roman society (portraits of Solon, of Philip of Macedonia and his son Alexander the Great, and Socrates). During the Roman age, portraits of illustrious Greeks belonging to the world of culture, philosophy and politics were often found not only in public buildings such as libraries or gymnasiums but even in some rooms of private homes.

ROOM VI
**Power and the Arts
The models
(*Exemplaria artis*)**
This room contains a series of terracottas, which although

13. Late-republican mosaic emblema portraying a cat and two ducks. From a suburban villa in the Cecchignola area

14. Head of Apollo in terracotta from the Domus Tiberiana. Augustan age

fragmentary, are of superior artistic quality. They were unearthed during the archeological excavations carried out in the Eighties, in the area of the *Domus Tiberiana*, one of the imperial palaces on the Palatine. They are exceptional exemples of the clay reproduction tecnique made from casts taken from classic period marble sculpture. These probably belonged to a workshop that dated back to the first augustan period, specialized in copies of original Greek pieces by famous artists from Magna Graecia (Pasiteles, Stephanos and Arkesilaos), as described by the writer Pliny the Elder. Artemis and Aphrodite, deities especially revered by Augustus, are also represented in this room.

ROOM VII
Power and the Arts
The originals (*Graecitas*)

The sculptures in this room come from the *Horti Sallustiani* (the area now known as the Ludovisi neighborhood), gardens which belonged to the Roman historian Sallust and before him to Julius Caesar. Several important original Greek sculptures were found here, imported after the Roman conquest of southern Italy, Sicily and Greece (between the III and the II century BC).
A masterpiece was discovered in this area and dates back to

about 440 BC; it depicts one of Niobe's daughters vainly trying to extract the arrow she was shot in the back with. The tale of Niobe's children, killed by Apollo and Artemis, is often the subject of ancient sculptures and paintings; in this case the sculpture must have come from the decoration on the triangular frontal of a Greek temple.
The statue of Pedagogue is a later figurative elaboration of the same myth. It depicts the companion of one of Niobe's youngest children and dates back to the IV century BC. The sculpture was placed in the *Horti Sallustiani*'s so-called "Ninfeo" and is perhaps a copy dating back to the Hadrian's age (II century AD).
A headless sculpture of a young girl dressed in a peplum (*peplophoros*) found in the area of the *Horti*, exhibits clean lines and refined workmanship and dates back to the V century BC. It shows an offerer whose effigy was originally dedicated in a sanctuary; the style reminds us of similar examples from Magna Graecia.
Undoubtedly, the most famous work discovered in this area during the end of the last century, and belonging to the collections of this Museum, is the so-called Ludovisi Throne (an altar depicting the birth of

Aphrodite, from about 460 BC, now almost certainly attributed to work produced in Magna Graecia). This work is on exhibit at the National Roman Museum located in Palazzo Altemps, together with the 17th century Ludovisi collection.

ROOM VIII
Power and the Arts
The figurative language (*Amoenitas artis*)

The works of art shown here are examples produced by sculptors belonging to the artistic tendency known as Neoattic, which was active from the end of the II century BC to the first imperial age.
These Greek artists were working in Athens or Rome itself, and the sculptures they created for their Roman clients were modified versions of either classical period (V - IV century BC) or hellenistic art (III – II century BC). The possession of Greek works or works of Greek inspiration was a powerful status symbol for the upper classes.
The inspiration for several statues of deities represented here can be found among great Greek statuary: an Athena (perhaps a statue of worship belonging to a temple on the Celio, and copied from an ionian original dating back to the V century BC), and an Aphrodite (copy done

15. *Statue of Niobid*
from Horti Sallustiani.
This sculpture represents
one of Niobe's daughters
falling, while she tries to
remove the arrow she
was shot in the back
with by the goddess
Artemis. It was part of a
group of sculptures that
illustrated the famous
myth of the Niobids,
who were killed by
Apollo and Artemis,
jealous of their mother.
The group probably
decorated the fronton of
a Greek temple, perhaps
the one of Apollo
Daphnephoros in
Eretria, Euboea. It dates
back to about 440 BC
and was probably one of
the original Greek
statues collected by
Caesar himself in his
gardens. This then
became the property of
the historian Sallust and
finally part of the
imperial domain

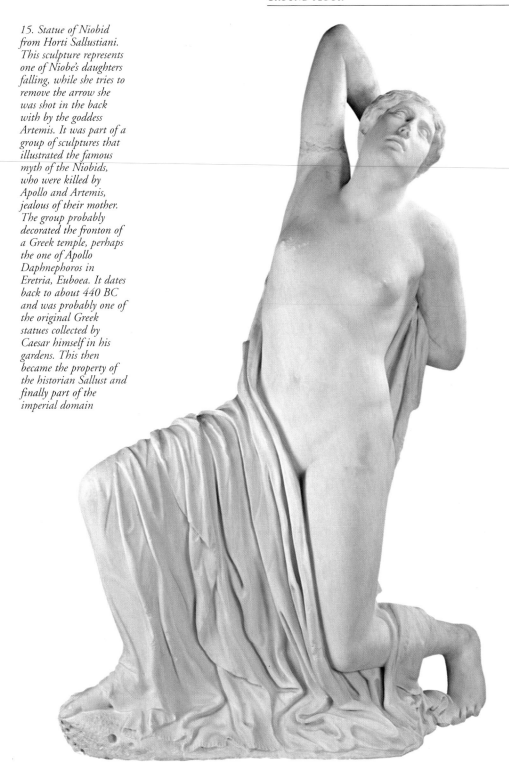

in the I century BC of one of the variations of Praxiteles' Cnidia, signed by the Greek artist Menophantos) and a Muse (a copy of the hellenistic original, after the type of Melpomene, with a tragic mask in her left hand).

Decorative examples are also on display here, and they include basins and furnishings for villas and gardens: a large cup with a group of marine figures; a base with dancing Maenads; an altar with Muses and Maenads, and several reliefs (one depicting a procession of Nymphs or Hesperides, and the other a frieze showing Nike leading a bull, probably inspired by the decorations on the Temple of Athena Nike in Athens).

Sculptures representing deities occupy the niches that run along the large staircase. All are copies inspired by classical and hellenistic works and were executed during the imperial age: a statue of Zeus from the villa of the Frerii in Tuscolo; a statue of Apollo from a villa along the Via Tiburtina; a statue of Dionysus with a cape around his hips, from the late-republican age villa of Voconio Pollione in Marino; a statue of the youthful Dionysus dressed in animal skin; a statue of a headless female dressed in peplum, perhaps Athena, and a draped idealized female form, also headless.

16. Statue of the Muse Melpomene, known as the Farnese type. I century BC. Copy of an hellenistic age original

17. Neoattic basin from the Hospital of Santo Spirito.
This large basin made of Greek marble, discovered on Lungotevere in Sassia, shows the excellence of execution and ornamental taste that characterized the work Greek artists made for their Roman clients at the end of the II century BC. Fashioned as a fountain, with water overlapping the edges, it presents a procession of marine figure, Tritons and Nereids, one of the most popular themes in Greek art

18. Base portraying dancing Maenads from the Sciarra Collection. I century BC. Modified copy of a Greek original from the late-classical age

FIRST FLOOR

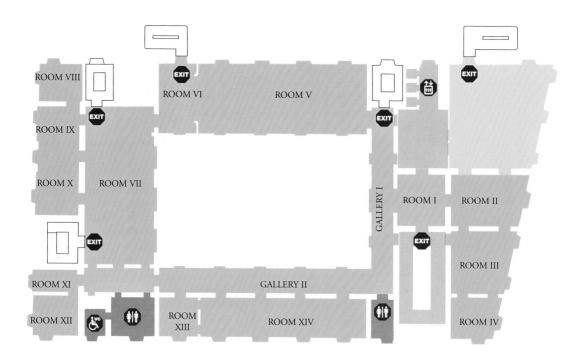

ROOM I
Image and celebration from the flavian period
(*Imago imperii*)

ROOM II
Image and celebration during the age of Trajan and Hadrian
(*Imago imperii*)

ROOM III
Image and celebration during the age of the Antoninians
(*Felicitas imperii*)

ROOM IV
Image and celebration during the age of the Antoninians
(*Felicitas imperii*)

GALLERY I
Portraits from Villa Adriana

ROOM V
Ideal sculpture represented in the imperial residences
(*Magistra graecitas*)

ROOM VI
Ideal sculpture in the gymnasiums
(*Ornamenta gymnasii*)

ROOM VII
Speculative culture Gallery of the deities
(*Simulacra deorum*)

ROOM VIII
Mythological cycles
(*Exempla virtutis*)

ROOM IX
Theater culture
(*Ornamenta theatri*)

ROOM X
Ornaments from the Ships of Nemi
(*Magnifica ornamenta*)

ROOM XI
Historical celebrations
(*Persuasio imperii*)

ROOM XII
Historical celebrations
(*Laus victoriae*)

ROOM XIII
Imperial iconography during the severian age
(*Imago imperii*)

ROOM XIV
Iconography and celebration from the Severi to Constantine
(*Laus auctoritatis*)

GALLERY II
Female portraits from the III and the IV century AD

The first floor exhibit consists of fourteen rooms and two galleries.

In rooms I-IV, XI-XIV and in the galleries, a series of portraits, reliefs and sarcophagi show the development of certain iconographic trends in official Roman art, and how the political and cultural horizons changed, starting with the flavian empire (end of the I century AD) and ending with the late empire (IV century AD).

Rooms V-X illustrate another very important aspect of Roman art between the I and the III century AD; the large number of bronze and marble statues being produced at that time were mostly inspired, reelaborated by Greek statuary of the V and the IV century BC and the following hellenistic period. Many of the works on exhibit were excavated at the same sites.

ROOM I
Image and celebration from the flavian period (*Imago imperii*)

The portraits in this room, which date back to the flavian dynasty (emperor Vespasian 69-79 AD, his sons Titus, 78-81 AD, and Domitian, 81-96 AD) once again demonstrate how portraits done at this time were used to promote the concept of imperial authority, even when tinged with benevolent "bourgeois" realism, (particularly evident in Vespasian's portraits).

Domitian's portrait, with its oakleaf crown (known as *corona civica*) is one of the few remaining portraits of this emperor. All images of him were destroyed by decree (*damnatio memoriae*) after he was killed during a palace conspiracy.

The statue-portrait of Julia, Titus' daughter, whose face shows an extremely refined naturalism, and a female portrait, identified as Domitia, Domitian's wife, testify to the evolution in feminine hair-style of the period, made of a high coronet with rows of curls and a plait rolled into a bum.

The emperor Nerva (96-98 AD) belonged to the old senatorial nobility and pursued the policy of restoring authority to the Senate. Here he is clearly portrayed as be-

in the previous page:

19. Statue-portrait of Giulia, Titus' daughter. From the Isola Tiberina

20. Portrait of Vespasian.
Two distinct themes run through portraits depicting the emperor Vespasian: the official and honorary, which is characterized by idealizations of the facial features; and the

more private one, •
marked by greater realism. This portrait, discovered in the Tiber, belongs to the second group and the massiveness of this old military leader's facial features betray his peasant origins

ing severely noble and vigo-
rous.

ROOM II
**Image and celebration
during the age of Trajan and
Hadrian (*Imago imperii*)**
Starting with Nerva, the
problem of imperial succession was solved by a system
that allowed for the adoption
of members from outside of
the family circle, thus allow-
ing leaders to be chosen from
among the best of the sena-
tors. Wars of conquest and
those which led to the stability of the provinces and borders allowed the Empire's citizens to enjoy a long period of
peace, good administration
and prosperity. The policies of
the emperors Trajan (98-117
AD) and Hadrian (117-138
AD), both military men and
natives of Spain, led to the
establishment of firm political, administrative and cultural relations between the capital of the Empire and its
provinces. In fact it was under
Trajan's reign that the empire
reached its maximum point
of expansion. The inscribed
bronze tablet exhibited in this
room is an extremely important document: it's the *tabula
alimentaria* of the *Ligures
Baebiani*, and demonstrates
the fiscal initiative which Trajan instituted in favor of the
social class of small land owners and the education of chil-

*21. Portrait of Sabina.
Portraits of Hadrian
and his wife Sabina
showed the trend
towards classical styles
that distinguished all the
art forms of that time.
This fine portrait of the
empress, veiled and
therefore considered to*
*be subsequent to her
death and deification,
shows the strong
influences that ideal
faces of great Greek
statuary had on the
Hadrian's period*

official portraits were used to promote a particular image of the ruling class. Portraits of private citizens done during this time drew inspiration more and more from the iconography of the imperial couple.

The style prevalent during this period is a synthesis between hellenistic naturalism and the traditional realism found in mid-italian art of republican age. The development of this style which can truly be defined as Roman, undergoes a change of direction however, and nears classical and hellenistic ideals during the reign of Trajan's successor and cousin, Hadrian. The bust of the emperor and the two portraits of his wife Sabina, and even the portrait of Antinoo, the young from Bitinia loved by the emperor, demonstrate the continuing idealization of human features in official portraiture.

ROOM III
**Image and celebration
during the age
of the Antoninians
(*Felicitas imperii*)**
During the reign of Hadrian's designated heir, *Titus Aurelius Antoninus* (138-161 AD), named *Pius* for his religiosity and his respect for public institutions, the Empire enjoyed an exceptional period of peace and stability. Since the

dren, known as *Institutio Alimentaria* (99 AD).
The portraitists' task, at this time, was to delineate and celebrate the emperor's wisdom, energy and temperance.

The statue-portrait of Trajan, dressed as the hero Hercules, and the beautiful portrait (from Ostia) of his wife Plotina, shown in this room, are interesting examples of how

*22. Head-portrait of
Antinoo with crown as
an hellenistic derived
iconography. From the
sanctuary of the Magna
Mater in Ostia*

emperor's sons, born by his wife Faustina Maggiore, had died, he adopted as his successors Lucio Vero and Marcus Aurelius, who was his daughter Faustina Minore's husband.

Official portraiture during emperor Antoninus Pius' long reign reflects the beneficial effects of a peaceful political and social climate. This period will be remembered in Roman history as the 'happy age' (*felicia tempora*). In the Roman art world, artists of Greek-Oriental origin dominate the scene and great technical competence lends an air of refinement to all the work produced during this time.

In portraits, statues and reliefs, the contrast between the color of hair, beard and clothing and the smoothness of the face is accentuated. This character of style can be seen in a selection of portraits of Antoninus Pius, his wife Faustina Maggiore and his daughter Faustina Minore. They are also evident in several portraits of unknown private citizens, in which physiognomy, expressions and hairstyles clearly refer to those of the reigning family. An excellent example of official portraiture is the statue of Antoninus Pius, posed in heroic nudity, from Terracina: here the theme of the nude figure, derived from the heroic Greek statuary of the V century BC,

is most successfully expressed. In this room there are also two important reliefs that have been identified as the personifications of the provinces of Thrace and Egypt.

They came from Palazzo Odescalchi in Rome but originally must have decorated a public building in Campo Marzio, possibly the Temple of Divus Hadrian.

23. Head-portrait of Antoninus Pius from Formia

24-25. *Two reliefs with personifications of the Provinces.*
The two provinces personified here have been identified as Thrace (the barefoot figure in a cloak, with a tunic uncovering the right breast, and a sword in her hand) and Egypt (the shod figure dressed in a tunic and fringed cloak, with a head-covering made as a band and decorated with rosettes).
They come from Palazzo Odescalchi, where they were installed after their discovery in Campo Marzio during the 17th century, near the site of the Hadrianeum, the temple of Divus Hadrian constructed in 145 AD by Antoninus Pius in honor of his predecessor. The reliefs, which have 17th century's elements added to them, belong to a series of twenty one panels that were decorated with personifications of provinces, and nine others which showed military trophies. These panels were discovered at different times, starting with the 16th century, in areas adjacent to the temple, whose archeological finds include part of the cella wall and eleven columns from the peristasi.

These reliefs originally alternated between personifications and trophies and formed a long frieze. Of these, seven depicting provinces and three with trophies are found in Palazzo dei Conservatori in Rome; others are dispersed among various collections.

Scholars disagree as to their original location. Several think they decorated the external podium of the temple, others say they were part of the interior wall of the cella and others hypothesize that they decorated another official monument from the antoninian age that

was situated in the area. This series of personifications illustrate a change of point of view in Roman art. In the I century BC the provinces were depicted as a source of trophies and prisoners (provinciae captae) but this frieze represents the provinces as an integral

part, support and keeper of the Roman empire (provinciae piae fideles), sharing in the same atmosphere of peace and general prosperity granted to all the Emperor's subjects.

Room IV
Image and celebration during the age of the Antoninians (*Felicitas imperii*)

During the age of Marcus Aurelius (161-180 AD), who reigned together with his adopted brother Lucio Vero (161-169 AD) for several years, sculpture begins to show elements of sentiment, particularly in portraiture. The emperor is also a philosopher and follower of the Stoic doctrine, therefore portraits of him and most masculine portraiture of this period try to create the model of a new man of action, filled with philosophical ideals (*homo spiritualis*).

Two of the portraits present in this room, perhaps of philosophers, are quite similar to the representations of Marcus Aurelius and are examples of the prevalent iconography found even in the portraiture that is not connected with the reigning family.

The two portraits of Lucio Vero clearly indicate the idealization of somatic features and an almost 'baroque' softness of style which distinguishes much work from this period. These elements are also evident in the statue identified as Lucilla, Marcus Aurelius' sister, and Lucio Vero's wife.

The portraits of Commodus (189-192 AD), Marcus Aurelius' son and the last of the Antoninian emperors, show the stylistic characteristics of the art during this period in its most 'baroque' form.

Gallery I
Portraits from Villa Adriana

From among the portraits shown in this gallery (all of them discovered in the area of Villa Adriana, the palace the emperor Hadrian had constructed near Tivoli), only two date back to Hadrian's age and express the classical tastes of the time. One is the portrait of a woman whose hairstyle was in fashion during Trajan's and Hadrian's age, and the other is the head of a barbarian.

The other portraits show clearly that the whole architectonic complex continued to be in use after Hadrian died. In particular, the fine portraits of emperors Antoninus Pius and Marcus Aurelius demonstrate, through the melancholy expressions on their faces, the aristocratic trends typical of Antoninian iconography.

The character of equilibrium and purity of art at that time is also evident in the portrait of a young girl, identified as Crispina, Commodus' wife.

26. Portrait of Caracalla from Villa Adriana.
This portrait is typical of one of the most widespread types done of the emperor, well known for his cruelty. The frowning and ferocious expression, the rendering of the facial features with their exaggerated heaviness and the contracted musculature of the subject were all intentional. This portrayal of the mature Caracalla shows an evident break with the previous stylistic trends of the antoninian age, still present in youthful representations of this emperor

Room V
**Ideal sculpture represented
in the imperial residences
(*Magistra graecitas*)** ·
The sculptural decoration
found in the holiday villas
was not very different in typology and function from the
one that adorned urban residences, imperial palaces or
home of the well-to-do. However, a villa outside of the city,
with its ample space and gardens and reconstruction of
buildings of a particular character, offered the ideal place
in which to exercise the pas-
sion for collecting, dear to
many owners. This phenome-
non brought about an in-
crease in the production and
circulation of sculpture, and
the artists liberally reworked
and copied ancient Greek
works from the classical and
hellenistic periods. Destruc-
tive excavations and probes in
villas throughout Lazio and
Campania that began during
the Renaissance and increased
during the 18th century,
made an abundance of works
of art available to museums
not only in Rome but in all of
Europe. Notable among the
core of the most important
discoveries that found their
way into the collections at the
National Roman Museum are
the works that originated in
Roman and Lazial villas
which belonged to the emperors, or those private ones
which later became imperial

property. Among these, Villa
Adriana in Tivoli and Nero's
villas in Anzio and Subiaco
played a special role as atte-
sted to by the sculptures on
display in this room.
In Nero's spectacular villa in

Subiaco the following sculptures were found: the head of
a sleeping girl which is possibly a sleeping Ariadne or a dy-
ing Niobid, and a headless
statue of Efebus, which also
belongs to the sculptural

27. *Statue of Efebo from
Subiaco.*
*This sculpture comes
from excavations of the
large terraced villa that
emperor Nero possessed
in Subiaco and dates
back to the I century
AD, but the modeled
base was added on a*

*later period. Inspired by
an original bronze, most
likely from the
hellenistic age, it shows
a youth falling down
and leaning on one
knee. The statue
probably represents one
of Niobe's children, and
was part of a larger*

*composite sculpture
depicting the slaying of
the Niobids by Apollo
and Artemis. These
sculptural group testifies
the propagation of the
Niobids' myth; they
decorated and animated
the spaces in the gardens,
grottos and niches of the*

*luxurious villas
belonging to the ruling
class*

28. Statue of a young girl from Anzio. Discovered in a niche of a gallery overlooking the sea in the emperor Nero's magnificent villa in Anzio, this sculpture is composed of two different types of Greek marble which were worked separately before being joined together. It's a technique that was wide-spread during the hellenistic age; in fact scholars agree to interpretate the statue as an original hellenistic work from the III century BC. It depicts a young delicately featured girl whose clothes are fluttering in the wind. She bears a tray containing objects that are probably connected with the dionysian cult and she most likely represents a priestess or an initiate

29. *Statue of Apollo from Anzio.*
The god Apollo is represented here as a youth in languid repose, his arm leaning on a support that at one time must have been a tree trunk with a snake wrapped around it. His wavy hair is bunched on top of his head, introducing a feminine element into this deity's iconography. The work, dated to the I century AD, was inspired by an original from the IV century BC, perhaps done by a sculptor who belonged to Praxiteles' circle. Imperial Roman artists often took into account the contexts and the places which were to be decorated and fashioned images of Apollo accordingly

group which portrays the Niobids as they try to elude Apollo's and Artemis' arrows. In the Imperial maritime villa at Anzio, whose apogee coincided with the neronian age, these statues were found: a beautiful young girl offerer which might be an authentic hellenistic sculpture of the III century BC, a statue of Hermes and one of Apollo and a group of Amazons on horseback swarming over a Galatian warrior. With the possible exception of the statue of the girl, all of these are Roman works inspired by the original Greek art of the V and the IV century BC.

Emperor Hadrian's residential complex in Tivoli, known as Villa Adriana, is the largest of the known Roman villas and the richest in furnishings and sculptural decorations, which now are found in many museums and European collections. Here we find: a statue of Dionysus; a valuable marble replica of a crouching Aphrodite by Doidalsas, the bronze original dating back to the III century BC; a statue of Athena; a statue of a young girl also known as the "Danzatrice di Tivoli" (Dancing girl of Tivoli), a marble crater with a crane and snakes; a grey marble frieze decorated with Centaurs; an Amazon's head, a copy of the famous original done by Phidias (V century BC) and a portrait of

30. Statue of Aphrodite crouching.
This statue, representing Aphrodite crouching, comes from the thermal area of Villa Adriana in Tivoli and is a prime example of artistic quality of the copies from Greek sculpture

produced in this emperor's age. It expresses the carnality of the goddess as she crouches and performs her ablutions. The original was a III century BC hellenistic bronze attributed to Doidalsas of Bitinia.

This type of statuary, refined and sensuous, was highly suited for the decoration of gardens, fountains and thermal baths, and the variety and number of its copies testifies to its popularity in the Roman world

Antinoo, the youth loved by Hadrian and honored as a god by the emperor after the boy's untimely death.

ROOM VI
Ideal sculpture in the gymnasiums (*Ornamenta gymnasii*)

The selection of sculptures in this room concern the iconography used in the decoration of gymnasiums, which were usually located in the gardens of large Roman villas. Both intellectual training and physical activity were carried out in these location. The exhibit begins with the statue named "Apollo del Tevere" (Apollo of the Tiber). The work is executed in an eclectic style inspired to a classical prototype usually attributed to Phidias, done in bronze and showing the deity in repose, as if to underline his role as peacemaker and benevolent protector.

Other statues representing deities in this room are a headless statue of Heracles, copied from the original that dates back to the IV century BC and two heads of Apollo Lyseum, copies of a famous statuary type created by Praxiteles for the Lyceums of Athens in the IV century BC. The statues of ephebi and athletes represented here are copies of those made by Polyclitis of Argo in the V century

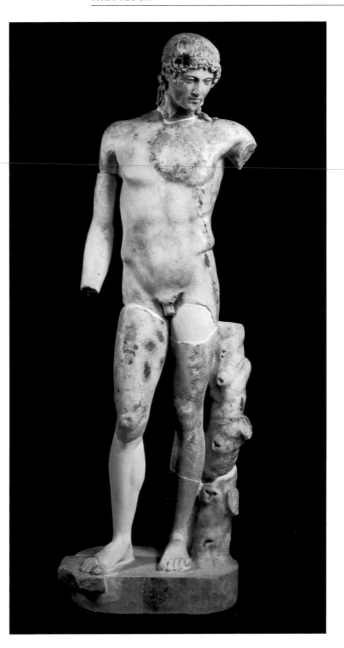

31. Statue of Apollo of the Tiber.
This statue of Apollo was discovered in the riverbed of the Tiber while works were being done on the embankments, and the surface erosion is due to the length of time it *remained under water. This representation of the god, serene and youthful, is represented according to the stylistic influences of the first classical age and shows influences from Phidias and Calamide's works. The original, however,* *was probably done during the augustan age by a neoattic artist. The iconography is incomplete since Apollo, when presented in the guise of a beneficent and peaceful god, is usually portrayed with a bow in his right hand* *and a laurel branch in his left*

32. Statue of the Discobolus Lancellotti. Discovered on the Esquiline in the 18th century this sculpture first became the property of the Massimo family and subsequently Massimo Lancellotti. It was sent to Germany during II World War and returned in 1948. It is one of the most famous of the Roman copies done of great V century BC Greek works, and faithfully reproduces an original bronze from about 450 BC which depicts an athlete in the act of throwing a discus. Historical tradition attributes this work to the sculptor Myron, who was well known for his portrayals of athletic figures in motion. This copy, which shows the not quite perfect three-dimensionality of the original, was done during the antoninian period (middle of the II century AD)

BC and Lysippus of Sicione during the following one, sculptors who specialized in these subjects.

The exhibit includes two copies of famous works of art from the II century AD: the "Discobolus Lancellotti", and the "Discobolus of Castelporziano" both realized in the V century BC by Myron. The first, attributed to the antoninian period but restored during the 18th century, is considered to be the reproduction most faithful to the original bronze because of its relative flatness. The original is dated about 450 BC and was highly regarded by ancient writers since it was one of the fundamental works of art that portrayed the figure of the athlete in motion. This motif was later repeated in the classical period.

The second reproduction, which is headless, was copied from the same myronian original and was discovered in 1906 among the ruins of a villa of imperial age in the royal estate of Castelporziano. It represents a more naturalistic and evolved version of the former.

ROOM VII
Speculative culture
Gallery of the deities
(*Simulacra deorum*)
Archeological discoveries demonstrate the widespread

use of sculptures that represented deities from the classical pantheon. These works were in marble and sometimes in bronze and they were either life-size or slightly smaller. The Romans not only showed a preference for Apollo, Artemis, Aphrodite, Dionysus, Athena and Heracles, but also for deities from

the secondary pantheon, such as those belonging to the Dionysian entourage. Aphrodite, the deity associated with water, was often represented at the thermal baths and in Roman gardens where the use of water was an essential part of the architectural scheme.

Several of the sculptures on

33. Bronze statue of Dionysus.
This statue was found while works were in progress on the embankments of the Tiber and given the scarcity of large bronze sculpture, this piece is particularly valuable.

Dating from the Hadrian's age (II century AD), it presents a refined and decorative example of the styles used in the representation of Apollo and Dionysus during the classical period. In this case, identification of

the god is assured by the hair style, which includes a crown of grape leaves, and the presence of the thyrsus, typically related to the dionysian cult, on which the figure leans with his left hand

display in this room come from extremely important residential estates. Two of these works, Artemis and Apollo Citaredo, were found at the Villa dei Quintili, on the Via Appia.

Images of the young Dionysus were commonly copies done from originals that date back to either the IV century BC or the hellenistic period. The favorite spots for these works were in gardens or living areas and they were often accompanied by other figures from the god's retinue, such as Pan, musical Satyrs and Maenads, or personalities from the theatrical world that were somehow connected with Dionysus. As for the famous statue known as the "sleeping Hermaphrodite", most likely inspired by a hellenistic original, its popularity was well documented by the large number of copies in circulation. The replica shown here is one of the finest known and comes from a luxurious private residence that dates back to the II century AD.

As for the realm of pleasure, innumerable copies of statues and paintings of Aphrodite and her companion Eros decorated the Roman villas and gardens.

At the far end of the room there are two sculptures of deities from the II century AD that were discovered along the Via Appia, in the township of Castel Gandolfo. The female statue, in peplum, might have represented Hera and was copied from a V century BC Attic original. The statue of a bearded Dionysus with a long chiton is a copy of a V century BC bronze, of the Dionysus-Sardanapalo type, which was worshipped in the eastern regions. The sculpture was originally headless but Mussolini had one added on in 1943, since he had decided to donate the statue to Nazi Germany as a symbol of the Nietzche-Dionysian cult. It remained in the city of Weimar from 1944 until 1991, when it was returned to Italy.

ROOM VIII
Mythological cycles
(*Exempla virtutis*)

The sculptural works on display here have themes taken from mythology and include decorations from metope and pediments of temples.

The torso of the Minotaur and the virile torso, probably discovered at the same site,

34. Statue of sleeping Hermaphrodite.
This statue, discovered among the ruins of a peristyle belonging to a private urban building, is a II century AD copy of a hellenistic original dating back to the II century BC. The figure, *endowed with attributes of both sexes, is reclining languidly on its right side on top of a draped slab which originally may have rested on a stone cushion. The multiple symbolic meanings inherent in the cult of this* *ambiguous figure were probably of little interest to the Roman clients, primarily attracted by the refined sensuality of this type of statue and how aptly it fit into the decorative scheme of exedras and gardens*

might have been part of a group representing the hero Theseus confronting the Minotaur. Both works are copies of Attic originals from the first half of the V century BC.

Achilles supporting a wounded Amazon (Pentesilea), derives from a hellenistic original from Pergamum and probably dates back to the II century BC.

The virile torso is a copy of part of a group statue, which probably may have been in bronze and which showed Odysseus-Ulysses stealing the Palladium (the sacred image of Athena) from the fortress of Troy.

ROOM IX
Theater culture
(*Ornamenta theatri*)
Among the works on exhibit here, which have to do with deities that are connected to the theater, we find several bearded hermae of Dionysus and Hermes done in archaistic style. Originally these had religious significance but then were mainly use for decorative purposes. The statue of the actor masked in the guise of Papposileno is one of many copies of this type and comes from a maritime villa in Torre Astura. This and other figures from Dionysus' retinue were often found in Roman villas. The two mar-

35. Statue of an actor wearing the mask of Papposileno, mythical father of the Satyrs and Dionysus' teacher. From the coastal villa of Torre Astura, in Lazio

ble slabs however, one decorated with the faces of Polyphemus and Galatea and the other with the head of Dionysus, come from a theater that was located in the woods belonging to the sanctuary of Diana in Nemi. Most likely they were originally placed on small pillars and columns similar to those found in the gardens of the houses of Pompeii. Theatrical masks and faces from Dionysus' circle (Satyrs, Maenads, Pan) were often used in this way. An atmosphere of dionysian sacredness was often achieved through the use of these elements in both theaters and gardens.

ROOM X
Ornaments from the Ships of Nemi (*Magnifica ornamenta*)

On display in this room are bronze ornaments that belonged to two ancient ships salvaged from lake Nemi, first in 1895 and then in 1932 (the two ships were subsequently destroyed during the II World War). Well rigged and richly decorated, they were probably used (as was also the custom in hellenistic courts) for banquets and feasts that were held on the lake by the emperor Caligula (37-41 AD), who had a villa on the shore.

The bronzes consist of a series of feral 'protomi' (heads of wolves, panthers and lions) and forearms which may have been part of the decoration on the ends of the beams and on the helms. A balustrade was also found which had small pillars that held a double row of transversal bars with two-faced Dionysian hermae (Satyrs, Sileni and Maenads). Among these bronzes, which demonstrate how extravagantly residences (even imperial floating ones) were decorated, one stands out for its superior artistic quality. It's the head of a humanized Medusa, done in the hellenistic tradition and cast in solid bronze, with the details brought out and refined by the use of a burin. Its function is unclear: it could have been the terminal part of a stern bean or of a side of the prow. It might as well have belonged to the decoration on the pediment of a votive chapel found on one of the ships.

36. Two-faced small hermae with Maenads. Part of the decorations on a balustrade which portray figures belonging to Dionysus' retinue. From one of the Ships from Nemi

ROOM XI
Historical celebrations
(*Persuasio imperii*)
A few significant reliefs pertaining to official Roman art, starting with the first imperial period, are on display in this room.

The relief with Victory which decorates a trophy, is an example of archaistic representative augustan art that uses the theme of victory in order to propagandize the consensus won by Augustus after he defeated Marc Antony and Cleopatra at Azio (31 BC).

An interesting relief from Terracina showing a construction scene (possibly from the port itself of Terracina) in the presence of an important personage, has been variously attributed to either the late republican age or the Trajan's one.

A third relief, with a partial view of a decastyle temple, belongs with another fragment preserved in the Lateranensi collections; this was interpreted as either a representation of the temple of *gens Flavia*, thereby dating it back to the Domitian's age, or of the temple of Venus and Rome and therefore from Hadrian's time.

ROOM XII
Historical celebrations
(*Laus victoriae*)
Beginning with the flavian age, and for the duration of the II century AD, the theme of victory over the barbarians becomes particularly evident in Roman art, especially since the barbarians were mustering on the borders (*limes*) of the Empire and forcing the emperors into never-ending military campaigns of containment.

The grandiose sarcophagus in this room comes from Portonaccio on the Via Tiburtina and shows battle scenes between Romans and barbarians. On the front it has a complex battle scene with the central figure of an advancing Roman commander. He also appears on the cover in a series of biographical scenes. Perhaps the sarcophagus was made for the burial of a general who participated in the military campaigns of Marcus Aurelius (161-180 AD); the scenes are close in style, content and iconography to the reliefs on the Antoninian Column.

The iconography utilized on this sarcophagus from the late antoninian age can be found in historical reliefs be-

37. Relief showing scenes of building activity that may have had to do with the new routing of the Via Appia and the enlargement of the port of Terracina

ginning with the I century AD and this can be demonstrated by comparing the scenes on the sides of this sarcophagus with a relief showing legionnaires, which is dated either to the period of the Flavi (69-96 AD) or Trajan (98-117 AD). It retains in part the figures of three soldiers advancing in a cane field, evidently engaged in a military campaign.

Another relief, with the figure of a barbarian and parts of other figures, probably belonged to the frieze of an official monument which celebrated a victory along the Empire's borders.

ROOM XIII
Imperial iconography during the severian age (*Imago imperii*)

With Septimius Severus (193-211 AD), an emperor of African extraction, a new chapter opens in the history of dynastic successions. His portraits, and those of members of his family, bear a close resemblance to those of emperors of the Antonini, as can be seen in the bust from Ostia, shown in this room.

As for the portraits of his two sons, Caracalla (211-217 AD) and Geta (211-212 AD), as young men, they are hard to identify. Geta's portraits were largely destroyed following the *damnatio memoriae* de-

38. Portrait of Septimius Severus. This bust of Septimius Severus wearing an armour shows a refined use of drill in the hair and the beard, and a play of light and shadows which arises from the contrast with the polished surface of the idealized face. These stylistic characteristics are similar to those in vogue in the portrayal of the antoninian period. Septimius Severus aspired to legitimize his power through adherence to the policies handed down by the Antoninians; that is why many of his portraits show the same ascetic characteristics as those done of Marcus Aurelius, the philosopher-emperor

creed by Caracalla. Perhaps the statue of a youth in an apollinian pose is one of his few surviving portrayals.

Instead the portraits of the mature Caracalla show signs of an increasing interest in stronger and more moving expressions.

The colossal head of Severus Alexander (222-235 AD), the last of this dynasty and family, shows a stylistic change of direction: expressiveness gives way to firmness and a frontally posed hieratic elegance.

ROOM XIV
Iconography and celebration from the Severi to Constantine (*Laus auctoritatis*)

Military anarchy marked a good part of the period between the death of Severus Alexander (235 AD) and the establishment of the Tetrarchy under Diocletian (284-305 AD). Every time an emperor died, struggles broke out between military leaders scattered throughout the various provinces and representatives of the senatorial class in the capital.

During the reign of emperor Gallieno (253-258 AD), there ensued a temporary period of equilibrium between the various components of the empire's society. Social and political conflicts howe-

ver, were to be definitively resolved by Diocletian until the end of the century, when administrative reforms split the Empire into two parts, East and West, each entrusted to an Augustus.

The works shown in this room exemplify the changes of style and content that marked Roman art in the III century AD and the beginning of the following one. Although these show diverse stylistic trends, the prevalent

is the one leading to 'late-ancient' abstraction. Portraiture and friezes on sarcophagi destined for the burial of the well-to-do show that the upper classes now prefer to have themselves represented in an idealized way. Man detached from the mundane world (*homo spiritualis*) becomes the new model, and with this a desire to show that one has based one's life on the dominant philosophical principles in vogue. Even among por-

39. Detail from the front of the sarcophagus Mattei with Muses. Euterpe with the double flute is in the center, flanked by Talia with the comic mask and Melpomene with the tragic mask. Sited in the Basilica of *San Paolo "fuori le mura" from the end of the 15th century, it was subsequently transferred to Villa Mattei on the Celio*

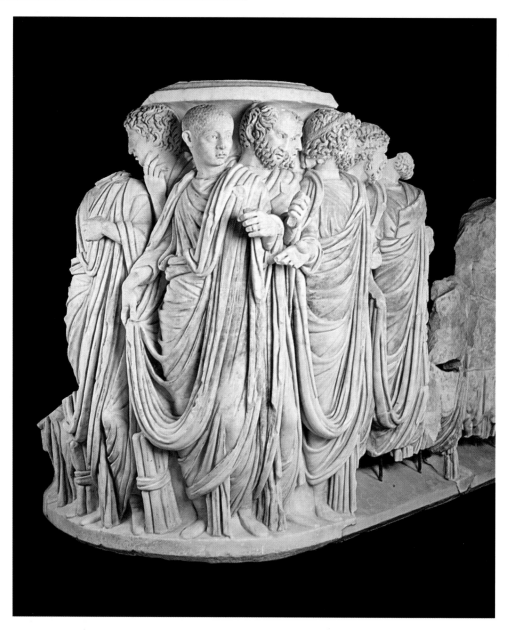

40. Sarcophagus from Acilia with a procession for the commissioning of a consul.
This sarcophagus is an excellent example of high quality artistic level of the funerary sculpture from the middle of the III century AD.
Although of a private nature, it was influenced by official art, as can be seen by the personification of the Roman Senate (Genius Senatus), the figure with toga and crown. The most convincing explanation for the scene portrayed is that it deals with a procession marking the commissioning of a consul, a ceremony which took place on the 1st of January. The consul is shown taking leave of his wife (who is followed by maidservants) and preceded by horsemen as he makes his way to the Campidoglio for the ceremony. The youthful figure situated in the left corner is probably the subject's son, who possibly died before his parents. The figures of a bride and groom, which occupied the center of the front of the sarcophagus, now mostly missing, had their right hands clasped together in a symbol of conjugal harmony

41. Sarcophagus of the Annona.
This sarcophagus, from the second half of the III century AD, must have belonged to someone holding the administrative office of Prefect of the Annona (praefectus Annonae), the highest position available to Roman Knights. In the center of the front of the sarcophagus we find the dead couple holding each other's right hand, in the presence of the personification of Concordia; to the sides there are four personifications which are identifiable, by means of inscriptions as well as attributes, as Portus (the port of Ostia), and Annona to the left, Abundantia and Africa to the right. The relationship between these four figures underlines the importance of wheat supply that came from the large estates of the african provinces. Arriving by sea at Porto, the wheat was then distributed under Anonna officials control, which had their offices in the city of Ostia

traits of private citizens the image of the emperor remains a constant point of reference, while on the sarcophagi the dead usually appears in the guise of a philosopher, often surrounded by the Muses.

One of the most illustrative examples of this trend in funerary art is the large sarcophagus with Muses from Villa Mattei, done in Greek-Oriental tradition and dated between 270 and 290 AD. A Muse occupies each of the niches except for those on the sides, which are filled by figures of philosophers.

The other two sarcophagi date back to the same period, and both are very close to the courtly style of official art. One shows the commissioning procession of a consul, from Acilia, and the other is known as the one "of the Annona". Both have effigies of the dead husband and wife surrounded by figures from their retinue and allegorical images.

The next works belong to the age of the Tetrarchy and Constantine, and once again artistic tendencies change. The courtly and classical forms are abandoned and naturalistic effects give way to pictorial ones with resulting expressiveness and immediacy. A somewhat more schematic but vivacious style characterizes reliefs and sar-

42. Small statue of Christ Teaching.
This statuette probably depicts Christ seated, with a roll in his left hand and his right hand extended. Classical sculpture typically showed philosophers in this pose. Although *dated approximately between the middle of the III century AD and the middle of the IV, therefore during the age of Constantine and the triumph of Christianity as the official Roman religion, this image of Christ Teaching is well* *documented from the many representations found on christian sarcophagi of the IV and the V century AD, thereby leaving little doubt about the identity of the work*

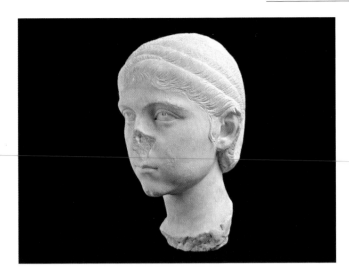

wife of Gordiano III (238-244 AD), one of Otacilia, wife of Philip the Arabian (244-249 AD), and one of an older woman, perhaps Etruscilla, wife of Decius (249-251 AD).

The portrait identified as that of Salonina, wife of Gallieno (253-268 AD), is executed in an accentuated classical style which was typical of the gallienic reign.

The crowned head of an older woman belongs firmly in the IV century AD, and testifies to the formal elegance and tendency toward rigidity typical of the period following the age of Constantine (306-337 AD).

cophagi. The sarcophagus of *Marcus Claudianus*, a member of the senatorial class (*vir perfectissimus*), constitutes one of the best examples of the artistic trends in vogue during the age of Constantine. Stylistically inspired by reliefs from the Arch of Constantine (315-316 AD) and decorated with episodes taken from the Old and New Testament, it clearly demonstrates how the new religion of Christianity had taken root during this time.

GALLERY II
Female portraits from the III and the IV century AD
As in preceding periods, the one bridging the reign of the Severi emperors (193-235 AD) and the age of Theodosius (379-395 AD) shows how female portraiture, unlike the male, represented its subjects in a substantially conservative style and how its subjects bore strong resemblances to images of women belonging to the imperial family.

Of note in this room, are the portraits of the wife of emperor Septimius Severus, the siryan Giulia Domna, and the wife of Caracalla, Plautilla, testifying the various hairstyles that were in vogue in the severian age.

The following group of portraits show the changing hairstyle, with a prevalence of braids drawn up on the head: a fine portrait which might be of Tranquillina, the

43. Head-portrait of Plautilla, Caracalla's wife

44. Head-portrait of Salonina, Gallieno' wife

SECOND FLOOR

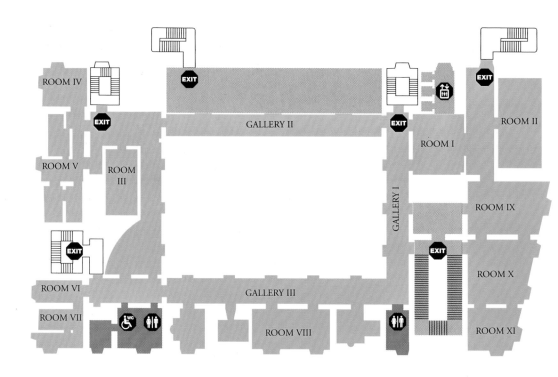

ROOM I
**Domestic decoration
during the I century BC**

ROOM II
**Triclinium with garden
paintings in Livia's Villa**

GALLERIES I and III
Mosaic floors

GALLERY II - ROOMS III - V
The Villa of the Farnesina

Gallery II
Cryptoporticus A

Room III
**Vestibule l, Triclinium C,
Corridor F-G, Garden L**

Room IV
Mosaics

Room V
Cubicles B, D, E

ROOMS VI-VII
**The Villa
of Castel di Guido**

ROOM VIII
**The Nymphaeum of Anzio
The Porto Fluviale
complex
The Hypogeum
of Aguzzano**

ROOM I X
The Villa of Baccano

ROOM X
**Megalografiae from the
late-ancient age**

ROOM XI
Inlay decorations

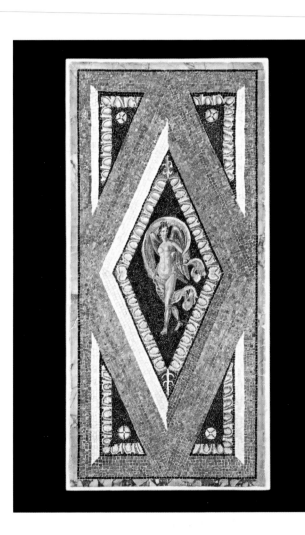

This floor contains some of the most notable groups of paintings, mosaics and stuccoes from the Roman art world and they clearly illustrate the degree of luxury achieved by the living rooms through the use of these decorative elements. Even though the frescoes that come from Rome and the Latial area cannot compete in number with those from areas such as Pompeii, Herculaneum and other centers in Campania destroyed by the eruption of Vesuvius in 79 AD, nonetheless Rome and its suburbs preserved pictorial cycles of exceptional importance and quality. Many of these can be found in this Museum's collection.

ROOM I
Domestic decoration during the I century BC

Among the rare examples preserved of pictorial art of the *domus* and villas of the I century BC in Rome are the ruins of a long wall, frescoed with scenes from the Odyssey, that belonged to a *domus* discovered in an excavation site on the Via Graziosa on the Esquiline during the last century. The fresco, probably dating back to the last phase of the republican age, was divided into a series of panels by architectonical perspective. Most of these panels found their way into the Vatican Library, except for the fragment shown here, which had been lost soon after discovery. The scene represents the encounter of Ulysses and the Sirens: he is lashed to the mast of the ship in order to resist the spell these birdwomen cast on the sailors with their songs, causing them to shipwreck. The landscape in which the scene is set shows some II century BC hellenistic influences, probably of alexandrine environment, and the work itself bears stylistic resemblances to frescoes (dated around 30 BC) belonging to the Pala-

tine house owned by Livia, Augustus' wife.

ROOM II
The triclinium with garden paintings in Livia's Villa

The writer Pliny confirms that a villa belonging to the wife of Augustus (27 BC - 14 AD), Livia Drusilla, was situated on the IXth mile of the Via Flaminia and was called *ad gallinas albas* in memory of an extraordinary event: an eagle was said to have dropped a snow-white hen bearing a laurel branch in her beak into Livia' lap. Once planted, this branch gave birth to the very forest that supplied Augustus and his successors with the laurel-wreath crown, symbol of the imperial triumph.

Excavations done during the last century unearthed a good part of the structures of this villa, including a statue of Augustus, now in the Vatican Museums, and the paintings with garden scenes, detached from their settings in 1951 because of conservation concerns, and transferred to this Museum.

The large room that contained these painted walls was semi-interred, covered by a barrel vault (only partially preserved) decorated with stuccos and reliefs. This was probably a summer *triclinium*; a large living and dining area protected from the heat. It was decorated with a re-

in the previous page:

45. Rhombus with Nike from the lacunar mosaic from Villa della Ruffinella in Tuscolo. End of the I century BC

46. Fresco with Ulysses and the Sirens, part of a pictorial cycle portraying scenes from the Odyssey. From a late-republican domus found on the Esquiline

*47. Detail from the
garden painting found
in the triclinium of the
Livia's villa*

*48. Detail from the
garden painting found
in the triclinium of the
Livia's villa*

fined representation of a garden (datable by style between 20 and 10 BC) which resembles other decorations found in Rome and in the area of Vesuvius.

Only two elements bear testimony to the presence of man: one is a cane fence in the foreground and the other is a low marble barrier which in the middle-ground forms small exedras. The rest of the wall is completely painted with illusionistic representation of a flourishing garden, replete with tall trees (spruce, cypress, pines and oaks), ornamentals (oleander, myrtle, boxwood and laurel) and fruit trees (pomegranate and quince). The lawn under the trees is filled with various types of flowers; the plants are all in full flower regardless of the season.

According to Pliny, this style was invented by *Ludius* (or *Studius*). Archeological studies however, reveal that this type of painting derived from hellenistic scene-painting, and represented the so-called Oriental *paradeisoi*.

GALLERIES I and III
Mosaic floors
The mosaic floors on exhibit along these two corridors date back to the time between the II century BC and the IV century AD. Some were discovered in the same archeological sites as the paintings on view in the Museum and others came from different areas not only in Rome but in all of Lazio and offer an ample panorama of mosaic art, which was often inspired by famous paintings.

Gallery I displays three finely executed mosaics floors from the *domus* of Priverno, that date back to the late republican age; the floor with rhomboidal figurated motifs comes from the villa of the Ruffinella, the panel (*emblema*) with fish comes from the Kircher-ian Museum and the floor with the basket of fruit still-life comes from a villa situated in Grotte Celoni, both in the hellenistic tradition.

In Gallery III there are important mosaics showing pygmies (from the area of the church of San Giacomo in Settimiana alla Lungara), a Nile-like scene (from the Aventine, closely related to alexandrian painting), and a large polychrome floor depicting dionysian *protomi* from the villa in Genazzano (antoninian age).

49. Mosaic emblema with basket of fruit and birds, from the Kircherian Museum. II-III century AD

GALLERY II - ROOMS III - V
The Villa of the Farnesina
These frescoes belong to a villa that was discovered on Lungotevere in 1879 during works being done on the river banks that edged the garden of the Renaissance Villa of the Farnesina. These are among the most important examples we have of Roman painting, and probably belonged to someone close to Augustus. It was hypothesized that Agrippa had the villa built for the wedding of Marcello and Julia (daughter of Augustus), and subsequently decorated when Agrippa wed the very same Julia, in 19 BC. Perhaps

abandoned in ancient times because of the Tiber's floods, only half of it was excavated and then promptly refilled. Frescoes from nine rooms, three stucco vaults and several mosaic floors were unearthed. The villa faced the Tiber in a large semi-circle perhaps with a portico, as did many of the coastal homes in Lazio and Campania.
The complex is an example of the richness and refinement of decoration present in the aristocratic homes at the beginning of the augustan age. Here one can find representations done in an architectonic style, which include mythological paintings typi-

cal of the so-called Pompeian "second style", landscapes and delicate paintings in the hellenistic tradition, continous friezes done in the Egyptian-like style and paintings containing slender architectonic elements that became known as the "third style".
It is evident how each living area had wall decorations that were adapted to the function of the room. Decorative motifs included symbolic and mysteric themes; here live together the archaistic, neoattic and Egyptian-like elements so popular in Rome at the end of the republican age.

50. Left wall of Triclinium C, with banner portraying vegetation and a scene of judgment

51. Left wall of Triclinium C, with landscape and frieze (at the top) showing a scene of judgment

Gallery II
Cryptoporticus A

The paintings on display here decorated an underground gallery (cryptoporticus), that was illuminated solely by basement window slits. The walls, which have a white background, are separated by columns, and in the spaces between are small pictures with landscape character and sometimes in a dionysian atmosphere, that is with images which refer to the cult of Dionysus.

Room III
Vestibule I, Triclinium C, Corridor F-G, Garden L

The paintings shown here belong to some passage areas (Vestibule I, Corridor F-G), reception (Triclinium C) and relaxation (Garden L).

The vestibule is painted with decorations on a red background, and displays a yellow baseboard decorated with grotesqueries. The triclinium, which faced an open garden and from which frescoed fragments depicting an ornate

in the previous double page:

52. Corridor F-G with figures of caryatids holding garlands. Landscapes and theatrical masks above

53. Detail of Corridor G with naval battle scene

54. Wall from the far
end of the alcove in
Cubicle B. Central
painting with infants
Dionysus and Leucotea

and festooned garden still remain, was once a huge room with a southern exposure. The painted walls, which had a black background, allow to presume that it was constructed for winter use. The frieze along the top part of the walls of the triclinium is narrative in character, with scenes of judgment in an Egyptian setting. In the middle ground evocative urban and country suggestive landscapes glow against the black background. Corridor F-G, partially curved, has a white background which is separated by caryatids that support slender architectonic elements. The upper part has small pictures of both dionysian and landscape character which show a rare freshness of execution and obvious hellenistic influences.

Room IV
Mosaics
Very few examples of mosaic floors were unearthed at the Villa of the Farnesina and all of them were geometric in nature. It is quite possible that if there were any polychrome paintings there, they would have been removed before the abandonment of the villa.

Room V
Cubicles B, D, E
These three cubicles, actually bedrooms, reconstructed in this room have vaults in their anterooms that are decorated with stucco. These vaults are divided into small landscapes and mystery-type paintings and are surrounded by an ornamental frieze that depicts vegetation and armed or sacri-

ficing Victories. The walls of the cubicles are frescoed in the so-called "second style", architectonically laid out with scenes painted in the niches. In Cubicles B and D the backgrounds of the walls are painted in cinibar; the first contains an exceptionally well preserved painting of the nymph Leucotea nursing the child Dionysus, and a beautiful section, done on a white background, of Aphrodite seated on a throne with a Cariti and young Eros. The latter uses a pictorial technique similar to the attical white-background *lekythoi* of the end of the V and the VI century BC.
The predominant decorative themes in these cubicles, with a great richness of themes, are related to the feminine world and erotism.

55. Detail from the left wall of Cubicle E. Central painting with sacred scenes

56. Detail from the stucco vault in Cubicle E. Central painting with Augustus in the guise of novus Mercurius

57. Detail from painted decoration in the "third style", with false architectures from the Roman villa of Castel di Guido

ROOMS VI-VII
The Villa of Castel di Guido

This reconstructed frescoed living quarter was in a suburban villa discovered on Via Aurelia, and, given the quality of the painted walls, it probably belonged to a high-born person of the Julius-Claudia age (first half of the I century AD). The room was covered with a barrel vault now lost, but still preserves a fine painted lunette framed with stuccoes. The three walls are architectonically partitioned in the manner of the "third style" and the couples Ares and Aphrodite, and Andromeda and Theseus can be picked out from among the mythological subjects.

ROOM VIII
The Nymphaeum of Anzio
The Porto Fluviale complex
The Hypogeum
of Aguzzano

The decorative groups here presented date back to the mid-imperial age (I - II century AD) and are related to particular contexts.

The so-called Nymphaeum of Anzio consists of a mosaic decoration on the walls (mosaics were not used exclusively for flooring) of an ornamental fountain discovered in the maritime villa of Anzio, which belonged to the emperor Nero. In this case shells, tesserae of glass and pumice were used as well as colored stones of various type.

This niche contains a naturalistic scene portraying a reclining Hercules, with Cupid for company, and a wild boar coming out of a grotto.

Porto Fluviale was a series of structures, perhaps destined for commercial use, connected to a dock on the Tiber and unearthed in the vicinity of the basilica of San Paolo, in the Pietra Papa zone. An entire frescoed room, dated back by brick stamps in the first antoninian age, and several fragments of painted walls from other rooms are on display here. The scenes have marine subjects on a cerulean background and include all kinds of boats in use along the rivers, with their helmsmen and oarsmen. The boats are surrounded by fish, molluscs and crustaceans that are depicted without regard to perspective. Over twenty species of marine life have been counted among these realistically painted sea creatures, all of whom were raised and used as food fish in ancient times.

The Hypogeum of Aguzzano is, instead, an underground funerary structure which dates back to the age of the emperor Hadrian. The inter-

58. Mosaic with bust of Dionysus.
This mosaic, most likely a floor, which is not datable by its architectonic context, contains a central emblema on a "bipedale" tile which depicts the bust of Dionysus-Bacchus as a youth, with the skin of a wild beast on his shoulders and a crown of vine branches and grapes around his head. This emblem is encircled by several polychrome bands decorated with various geometrical motifs. These motifs, (especially the wavy one), along with other stylistic characteristics, can be compared to similar ones on mosaics from Rome and the rest of Italy and help date this work back to the middle of the III century AD. The motif of the youthful god, however, appears on other mosaic floors from different periods and is even depicted in the famous group of mosaics from the villa of Piazza Armerina, in Sicily (IV century AD)

59. Ninfeo from Anzio,
in the area of the
imperial Villa.
Central niche with
representation of
reclining Heracles.
Neronian age

60-61. Frescoed
fragments showing
marine fauna.
From a complex,
possibly commercial, in
Pietra Papa, near the
fluvial port of San
Paolo.
First half of the II
century AD

nal walls, completely covered with a fine decoration in white stucco, were detached from the structure and brought to this Museum. Various decorations include: Dionysian subjects; those related to the myth of the birth of Helen and the Dioscures, hatched from an egg fecundated by Zeus; Romulus and Remus (the twins who founded Rome) being nursed by a wolf and lastly, the encounter between Mars and the vestal virgin Rhea Silvia. These decorations hold multiple symbolic meanings often associated with the funerary art of the aristocrats, and show the important role given to the legend of the founding of Rome.

ROOM I X
The Villa of Baccano

The floor from the villa excavated in the Baccano zone along the Via Cassia, comes from a vast residential complex belonging to the imperial Severi family. It is one of the most interesting of the III century AD villas of this type and originally consisted of a two-storey structure with a thermal bath on the lower floor and living rooms on the upper one. The huge floor, which is marine in nature, comes from the bath area and depicts a mask of Oceano in the center, surrounded by creatures from the sea. Another floor comes from an up-

62. Hypogeum of Aguzzano. Detail of the niche portraying the birth of Helen and the Dioscuri from an egg. Hadrian's age

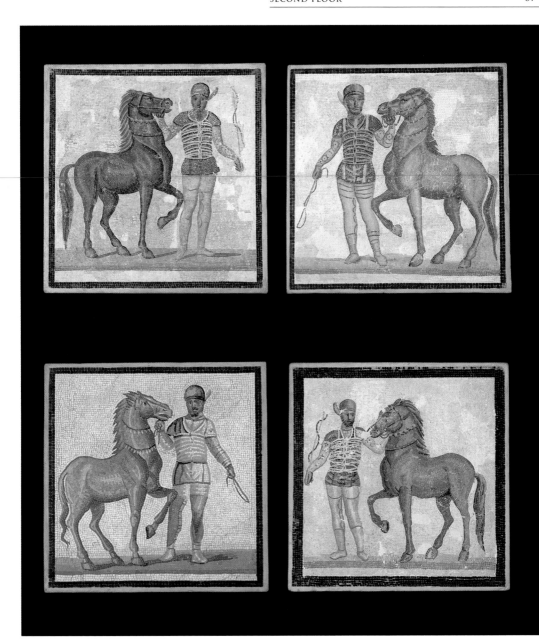

63. Emblemata with
four charioteers which
represent the factions of
the circus. From a villa,
probably belonging to
the imperial Severi
family, excavated in the
zone of Baccano on the
Via Cassia.
III century AD

64. *Fresco portraying*
Venus seated, restored as
Roma, known as "dea
Barberini". Excavated
in the 17th century in
a room near the
Baptistry of San
Giovanni in Laterano,
and since then part of
the Collection of

Palazzo Barberini.
First half of the IV
century AD

stairs cubicle and has four squares (*emblemata*), each of which has a charioteer representing the four factions of the circus (blue or *veneta*, green or *prasina*, red or *russata* and white or *albata*) with their horses. The third floor is a complex paneled composition consisting of thirty two surviving panels decorated with Muses, the Seasons and other mythological characters.

ROOM X
Megalografiae from the late-ancient age

The paintings shown in this room are rare samples of the III and the IV century AD Roman art works. These works have tended to drift away from a naturalistic form of representation and contain large figures in settings that have few formal architectonic devices (the so-called "megalografia"). One of the panels comes from a rustic villa situated in Casal Morena, on Via Latina, and dates back to the end of the III century AD or the beginning of the subsequent one. It shows two figures, perhaps the owner of the farm and his sharecropper. Shortly afterward (probably from Constantine's age, 306-337 AD) were done two frescoes: the one called "Dea Barberini" discovered in the17th century in Laterano, and the panels (later damaged by a fire)

where three figures can be seen, perhaps deities or members of the imperial family, together with a charioteer and sea animals. These panels belong to a pictorial cycle which decorated a corridor found in a villa in the area of the Laterano. The fresco with the "Dea Barberini" (already documented and lauded by Winckelmann), showing a female figure seated on a throne who probably personifies Venus, was restored and modified with the addition of a helmet and writings in the 17th century. At that point she was restored as the goddess Roma, which is not all that unusual since Venus was honored in Rome as the mother of Aeneas and therefore the Trojan progenitress.

ROOM XI
Inlay Decorations

The display in this room has excellent examples of a particular decorative technique (*opus sectile*) that involves the use of marble, stone and even colored glass cutted in slabs (*crustae*) of various forms and dimensions. Two panels, inlaid with vitreous materials, may have been a floor belonging to one of the formal drawing rooms belonging to a villa on the Via Cassia owned by the emperor Lucius Verus (161-169 AD). The valuable panel with the head of *Helios-Sol*, on the other

hand, was found under the church of Santa Prisca on the Aventine inside a Mithraic temple (a subterranean area of worship dedicated to the persian god Mithra). This dates back to the severian age (first decenniums of the III century AD). Two panels from the Basilica of Giunio Basso, consul in 331 AD, show the extraordinary luxury that characterized the private residences of the aristocratic urban class of the IV century AD. One of these contains the representation of the myth of Hylas abducted by the Nymphs and the other shows the beginning of a race at the circus. These panels in fact, along with two others now part of the collections at the Palazzo dei Conservatori, belonged to the decorations found on the wall of a large hall which was the private basilica in a luxurious structure sited near the Esquiline. The existence of an inscription allowed for its identification as the property of the consul Giunio Basso, father of the Roman prefect of the same name. The latter, a christian, died in the year 359. Discovered during the 15th century, the hall was subsequently destroyed, but all of the panels in opus sectile were seen and drawn by the well-known Renaissance artist Giuliano da Sangallo, who described them as "cosa meravigliosa" (a thing of wonder).

65. Inlay of Helios-Sol from the Mithreum of Santa Prisca.
This panel is inlaid with limestone and various types of colored marble and was made during the severian age (first decenniums of the III century AD). It was found in a mithreum, an underground temple dedicated to the cult of the persian god Mithra. It was not unusual to find images of the solar deity Helios-Sol in these temples, as often as not placed above the niche containing the statue of Mithra killing the bull. The god's face, depicted with notable technical skill, has shading obtained by firing, a technique that connects it to representations found in hellenistic Greece of Alexander the Great, which in turn is similar to Helios.
The cutting of marble slabs (crustae) for use in the decoration of floors and walls began in the Orient during remote times, and had already spread to Rome and to Italy by the republican age, but this technique, used for figurative compositions not only for geometric ones, was employed particularly during the I century AD under the reigns of Claudius (41-54 AD) and Nero (54-68 AD).
This kind of decoration enjoyed immense popularity until the late Empire, yet few examples remain. This is because these works were much in demand during the Middle Age for their marble, which was pillaged and re-used in other ways

*66. Panel in opus sectile
from the so-called
Basilica of Giunio Basso.
Detail of a Nymph from
the scene of Hylas'
abduction*

67-68. Panels in opus
sectile from the Basilica
of Giunio Basso.
These two panels,
consisting of inlaid
colored marbles, hard
stones, vitreous pastes
and mother-of-pearl are
valuable examples of the
decorative mosaic
technique known as opus
sectile.
These works were part
of the wall decorations
in the large meeting hall
of a building situated on
the Esquiline, that,
according to an
inscription, belonged to
Giunio Basso, consul in
the year 331 AD. Two
other panels, now in the
comunal collections
of the Palazzo dei
Conservatori, depict
tigers biting several
calves and come from

the same site.
One of these panels
depicts the abduction of
the youth Hylas, near a
spring, by the Nymphs.
The youth is rewarded
with immortality and
the myth refers to the
transcendence of the
soul. The other panel
depicts a chariot being
driven by an upper class
personage, probably
Giunio Basso himself,
followed by four
horsemen representing
the four factions of the
circus (veneta, russata,
albata and prasina).
These panels
demonstrate not only the
high degree of
refinement in
aristocratic residences
of this period, but also
the richness of symbolic
meaning and ideologies

in vogue in the Roman
upper classes of the IV
century AD. Not yet
converted to
Christianity, these
Romans still upheld
their pagan beliefs

BIBLIOGRAPHY

Pertaining to Palazzo Massimo and the surrounding area:

V. Massimo, *Notizie storiche della villa Massimo alle Terme Diocleziane,* Roma 1836.

R. Corsetti, *Il passato topografico e storico dell'Istituto Massimo alle Terme,* Roma 1898.

G. Matthiae, *La villa Montalto alle Terme,* "Capitolium", 14, 1939, pp. 139-147.

M.G. Barberini, *Rione XVIII. Castro Pretorio, I* (Guide rionali di Roma, 36), Roma 1987.

A.F. Caiola, *Da villa Montalto a piazza dei Cinquecento: i perchè di una distruzione,* in M. Barbera, R. Paris (a cura di), "Antiche Stanze. Un quartiere di Roma imperiale nella zona di Termini", Catalogue from the show (Rome, National Roman Museum, Thermal Bath of Diocletian, dicember 1996 - june 1997), Milano 1996, pp. 192-210.

Pertaining to the collection belonging to the National Roman Museum:

R. Paribeni, *Le Terme di Diocleziano e il Museo Nazionale Romano,* Roma 1932 (2nd ed.).

B.M. Felletti Maj, *Museo Nazionale Romano. I ritratti,* Roma 1953.

S. Aurigemma, *Le Terme di Diocleziano e il Museo Nazionale Romano,* Roma 1970 (6th ed.).

A. Giuliano (a cura di), *Museo Nazionale Romano. Le Sculture, I, 1 - I, 12,* Roma 1979-1996.

I. Bragantini, M. de Vos, *Museo Nazionale Romano. Le Pitture, I, 1. Le decorazioni della villa della Farnesina,* Roma 1982.

Pertaining to the history and restoration of the National Roman Museum:

Roma Capitale 1870-1911. Dagli scavi al Museo. Come da ritrovamenti archeologici si costruisce il Museo, Catalogue from the show (Rome, National Roman Museum, Thermal Bath of Diocletian, september-november 1984), Venezia 1984.

Forma. La città antica e il suo avvenire, Catalogue from the show (Rome, Curia of the Roman Forum), Roma 1985.

Il Nuovo Museo Archeologico di Roma, Catalogue from the show (Rome, Palazzo Massimo alle Terme, 1989), Roma 1989.

M. Bertinetti, M.R. Di Mino (a cura di), *Archeologia a Roma. La materia e la tecnica nell'arte antica,* Catalogue from the show (Rome, National Roman Museum, Thermal Bath of Diocletian, april-december 1990), Roma 1990.

PHOTOGRAPHS AND PLANS

The photographs are from
Giorgio Cargnel, Giorgio
Colasanti, Romano D'Agostini,
Luciano Mandato of the
Soprintendenza Archeologica
di Roma.

2: from AA. VV., *Il nuovo Museo
Archeologico di Roma*, Catalogue
of the show (Roma, Palazzo
Massimo alle Terme, 1989),
Roma 1989, p. 9.

8, 50, 51, 52, 53, 54,
55, 56: Gian Piero Casaceli.

11, 12, 15, 27, 31, 33,
34, 59: Lorenzo De Masi.

37, 62: Maria Teresa Natale.

47, 48: Archivio Scala.

Electa Guides for the
Soprintendenza Archeologica
di Roma

Series edited by
Rosanna Cappelli

PALAZZO MASSIMO
ALLE TERME

Text
Marina Sapelli

Translation
Nora Kersh

Printed in 1998 on behalf of Elemond Spa
by Tipografica La Piramide (Rome)